Glimpses beyond the Mirror

Glimpses beyond the Mirror

Poems of Pilgrimage

Searching For What Lasts Past Today

Steve Kennedy

Although the author has made every reasonable effort to ensure that the information in this book is correct, the author does not assume and hereby disclaims any liability to any party for any loss, damage, or disruption caused by errors or omissions, whether such errors or omissions result from negligence, accident, or any other cause.

Copyright © 2023 by Steve Kennedy

All rights reserved. No part of this book may be reproduced or transmitted in any form or by any means, electronic or mechanical, including photocopying, recording, or any information storage and retrieval system, without permission in writing from the author.

ISBN: 978-1-6653-0675-1 - Paperback

This ISBN is the property of BookLogix for the express purpose of sales and distribution of this title. The content of this book is the property of the copyright holder only. BookLogix does not hold any ownership of the content of this book and is not liable in any way for the materials contained within. The views and opinions expressed in this book are the property of the Author/Copyright holder, and do not necessarily reflect those of BookLogix.

Library of Congress Control Number: 2023911503

⊚This paper meets the requirements of ANSI/NISO Z39.48-1992 (Permanence of Paper)

Scripture quotations are from the ESV® Bible (The Holy Bible, English Standard Version®), copyright © 2001 by Crossway, a publishing ministry of Good News Publishers. Used by permission. All rights reserved.

070623

*For those who have gone before,
and for all those yet to come.*

"The gross heathenism of civilization has generally destroyed nature, and poetry, and all that is spiritual."
—John Muir

"For those who weep will find, and to those who knock, the door will be opened."
—Luke 11:10

ix
Acknowledgments

x
Introduction

1
Back Then

Back to Sognefjord
Nasty, Brutish, and Short (I have had students)
From What Distant Place
Albrecht Altdorfer's *Alexanderschlacht*
Past That
Modern-Day Nancy Drew and Hardy Boys
When I Think Of
Light and Shadow
Plenty, and Not Enough
African American History Museum

24
Glimpsing Couples

Blueberry Fields Forever
The One I Failed
Sailing
Bedtime Story
Te Amo, I Love You, *Ich Liebe Dich*
The Things She Said

34
Perils and Pilgrims

Kennedy Meadows, Sierra Nevada
Life Is Not the Silver Comet

Where Have You Been, and Who Are You Becoming?
World Demise—Now What?
Creatures Come Calling
A Guide to Middle School, or Heaven and Hell
Desert Dreaming

46
Poetry for People

Poetry Is
Poem for Poets
Nursery Rhymes and a Broken World

53
Souls/Sanctuary

Skulls on Fence Posts
No Turning Back
Ash Wednesday
Gracious
37,000 Feet
Margin
Electing to Depart
Compromised Couriers

68
Beyond the Mirror

Ode to Superheroes
My Friend Chuck
At a Loss for Words
Looks and Souls
Long Road to Mortality
A Love Song for Beulah and Maida
Births and Deaths
Standing at the Fountains
Faces and Lights
One Day, Or 10,000—No Matter

Acknowledgments

Many people (some of whom have already departed) contributed to the making of this volume—family, friends, writers, and countless others.

Thanks to Chanel Moore and Ben Helton for reading, reviewing, and making suggestions , and to John Baskam for his constant encouragement.

Special gratitude goes to my wife, Barbara, and our loved ones scattered all around.

Introduction

Why poetry, and why now? Some of the world has "moved on" from this ancient genre to the internet and more fast-moving things. But there are reasons. As the intrepid explorer John Muir said long ago, "The gross heathenism of civilization has generally destroyed nature, and poetry, and all that is spiritual." The naturalist-writer knew mountains better than anyone, and he also knew how we humans forsake them—and beauty—and truth, for things of less value. Poetry can interrupt our busyness with shallow things, bring us back to what is real and true and beautiful, or what is heart-breaking or terrifying or confounding. Poetry has helped me to learn (again and again) about the world, and learn about myself; may this slim volume encourage you to do so too. This only happens if we are willing to open ourselves to the power behind what the verses have to offer.

Poetry—as with pain and ecstasy—can be very personal. Poetry is universal, just as pain and ecstasy inhabit every palace, hovel, and places in between. These poems might be new, but the earliest recorded poetry emerged at least four thousand years ago. Often, young and old can look askance at the myriad titles and names of poets from across the centuries. Nonetheless, my students often expressed surprise and even delight when they found (or created) poems that bring up some unknown longing or darkness from within. We mortals are birthed with the capacity and a yearning to express such deep feelings among ourselves and to the universe—and verse can often be the most concise and direct way to do so. Away from the riveting and unforgettable moments of childbirth or death, our minds are often spent looking back or looking ahead to those experiences or images that can brand our identity.

There are still empty spaces in the cosmos. They are gradually being filled up with cries of anguish or murmurs of love or distinctly different tones. It's also waiting for your contribution in whatever form. Sometimes those empty spaces are apparently being filled with a voice or voices from another realm. Many of these poems spring from different times of wonder, grace, regrets, or rejoicing that may seem to transcend the prosaic world—illumination from a giant medieval painting in a Munich museum, amazement at the sight of a grandbaby, startling sparks from class discussions, or literary and gory parallels popping up in nearby suburbia. It's not always easy for any writer to point out where or how a certain poem might have originated—just as much from without as from within. One thing is clear to me: there is more in your and my imagination that we can hardly conceive. Are you willing to seek what is there?

Most all of these selections were written as my children were becoming adults, getting married, and having children of their own. Looming over several of the poems are ancestors, parents, pictures and places from long ago, a lovely and supportive wife—plus a presence or presences better sensed through verse than described in prose.

All poets may not be as fascinating as the mystic William Blake, the pioneering Langston Hughes, the tortured soul of Rilke, or such iconoclasts as Whitman and E. E. Cummings. (This writer pales in comparison). Few of Emily Dickinson's contemporaries knew of her poetic imagination until long after she passed away. Neither John Keats nor Sylvia Plath achieved much recognition before their untimely deaths. Regardless of the kind of lives that such poets lived, their works light a way to territory otherwise uncharted. There are places and vistas that can only be reached in this way. Only the reader can tell if even a tiny flash or two shines from within this volume.

Why do poets write poems, and why do readers read them? There are likely more reasons than people. Possible reasons:

- Poetry can highlight key insights for both writer and readers.
- Poems can enhance self-awareness, focus observational powers, and heighten mindfulness.
- They can function as a place of confession, repentance, and grieving.
- A poem can help process wounds, bring healing, forgiveness, and even renewal.
- Some poems can instill perseverance, understanding of others, and humility.
- At its best, poetry can bring writers and readers into relationship and community.

If, in reading these poems, any of the above reasons is at least partly fulfilled, that is both your and my good fortune—as a matter of common grace.

Back Then

Back to Sognefjord

We were tired and impatient
On a long ferry ride from Bergen to Stavanger
When I met this older man who spoke English,
Which was a bit different, and his older wife.
We struck up a conversation—not easy with the taciturn
  Norsk—
And he told me he'd emigrated to the States to be a farmer
On a large ranch out on the Montana plain.
They'd raised a family, made a good life,
But after twenty years, that was over now.
His parents had died and the little
Farm on the fjord where he'd grown up was
His if he claimed it.
I looked out at the storm clouds and choppy waves,
No sign in this weather of the icy peaks
Just a few kilometers inland,
Trying to imagine his return to the tiny town
Tucked away from the North Sea
In the shadows of snow-capped mountains.
I still wonder . . .
Whether he stayed put there,
Toiling away on the mountainside,
Racking hay and milking the goats,

Listening to Hardanger fiddle tunes.
And if he did, were those days —
Herding cattle on horseback
With his teenage boys,
Shooting coyotes,
Going to town in his pickup truck
In Big Sky country just a dream?*

Norway

---

*Note: Sognefjord is the longest fjord in Norway. Bergen and Stavanger are two of the largest Norwegian cities. Hardanger fiddle is often used for traditional music in Norway.

Nasty, Brutish, and Short
(I have had students)

I have had students, far brighter lights than mine—even
    before fading,
Starting long ago—
Snuffed out before their time.
Whimpers in the classrooms, black ribbons in the hallways,
A long trail of those too young to the churchyard.

You shrug your shoulders, stare at the barren hills—
And move on.
When the odd pang arises inside,
Is it the chipotle or pork chop, or instead
The dread disease that took your grandmother almost
    eighty years ago,
And then your mother too?

Will you groan and wither like grass?
Eat ashes as your only food?
Roost alone among the ruins until the dark force comes?

Without redeemers, all of us perish—
Solitary, poor, nasty, brutish, and short.
Is the life measured out in mishaps and miseries
Instead of years?

At the surprising end of the tether,
Can you embrace surrender
To learn finally how to live?
When there's no time left,
Who wants a paradox then?

Embracing surrender
At the crossroads ahead,
Change our eyes, change our hearts.
Souls, do not rest.
Die to celebrate.

From What Distant Place

From what distant place
Can their grandmother pull these things?
   She sings from memory winsome nursery rhymes
And lullabies never heard for sixty years;
Tells ghost stories and campfire riddles
In the evening twilight.
Streetlights peek through the leaves and the blinds.
Little ones strain to keep their eyelids open and say,
"Do it again."

Albrecht Altdorfer's *Alexanderschlacht*

Back in the old days when it was nothing to
Walk into the Alte Pinakothek in Munich,
To stand in awe of Altdorfer's *Alexanderschlacht*,
Be pierced by the flaming sun descending into the dewy
   mountains,
And transfixed by the cosmic and the microscopic.
(A)historical, geographic, metaphysical views of
Alexander's defeat of Darius at Issus
East versus West, Asia against Europe—
A dizzying, dystopian rhapsody of Christianity's triumph
   Over "Oriental" religions, whether Persian
   Zoroastrianism or Ottoman Islam—
No relation to any map or world man has ever seen,
Except in the heavens
Where an invisible force holds aloft a Latin banner
Proclaiming the victory of a boy-prince in armor
Over a fleeing emperor and his tottering empire,
Hardly a sign of the innumerable deaths sure to come.
Battle-hardened soldiers, all steeled for death.
Of course, no women nor children clog this scene,
Though certainly millions of them have lain innocent
   victims
Across the centuries into today's headlines.

No kitchens, washtubs, or clotheslines disturb the view.
Look in vain for the mother
Changing a diaper for the baby,
In whose name the warriors war.†

---

† Note: Albrecht Altdorfer was a renowned painter during the German Renaissance, and his tremendous picture of *The Battle of Alexander at Issus* is now known as *Alexanderschlacht* (*Alexander's Battle*) and is in the Alte Pinakothek in Munich.

Altdorfer Alexanderschlacht Painting‡

---

‡ Albrecht Altdorfer, Historienzyklus: *Alexanderschlacht (Schlacht bei Issus)*, 1529, Bayerische Staatsgemäldesammlungen - Alte Pinakothek München, https://www.sammlung.pinakothek.de/en/artwork/9pL3Qyz4eb.

Past That

Years of it,
His sin ever before him,
Seizing every moment,
Deceiving, manipulating, ravenous.
Selling birthrights for a
Nanosecond of ecstasy,
Leaving behind boulevards of tears, broken promises,
Nightmares of betrayals, heart-shattered lives
Persisting in colossal self-condemnation.
A pit set loose among the dead,
A horror amid the darkness,
A dying inside and out before
Suffering much and causing more.
Miserable wretch washed ashore.
Could he, like some Nazi prison guard,
Say that he'd only been following orders
From his own twisted heart?
No use now—the poison's already slithering downstream,
Along with its victims slipping away for good.
There was a shedding of the skin that covered
Nakedness.
Longing for a deliverance from blood-guilt,
He wandered down broken alleys and twisted lives

Hoping his hands and heart would be pierced,
Seeking a place of suffering.
Confessions, of crimes of the heart and mind—
Who is he, and who is the one to save?
To redeem the two bits left from the sordid mess
Of years in shame?
A path away from the septic pool
Into the glistening forests,
A rescuing angel might point
Every once in a while.
How dare he look down on any living thing—
Death row, hyenas, June bugs—after all that was done?
It kept coming back to haunt:
A ghoulish face, the skeleton dripping,
Staring back from the mirror.
Now . . .
If there is just one Light,
He might snatch back the remains of the night
   Before all becomes darkness.

Modern-Day Nancy Drew and Hardy Boys

Back in the 1950s, what a comfort it was, that
Nancy always knew how to find out who did what.
No matter the perils, her persistence perennially
Paid off in ferreting out the who in whodunit.

What words can describe this sleuth?
Curious, persevering, kind, decent, sly even;
Reliable in detecting, even without a mom or sibling,
She earned our trust

Those Hardy Boys, though seemingly
So fresh-faced and plain vanilla,
Always followed up a lead,
Never shirked from challenging a cop
Who wasn't as interested in solving a mystery.
Wanted to know the truth and nothing but
The truth.

How sad that we know that Nancy was just
Made-up, a fairy-tale fable for
More naïve times, just like
Joe and Frank—fantasy caricatures from
The hack writers at the same publishing house.

All these myths for those long-ago days
When people needed to believe in something
(Since we don't anymore).
Maybe they were, and always will be.

Still, to look up to—
Who would move to Uganda at twenty-three and adopt
   thirteen orphans?
Katie Davis would and did.
That would be almost as crazy as
Walking into the Colombian jungle
To bring good news and more to a lost tribe.
Bruce Olson walked in and came out as
Bruchko, more persistent, more hardy.
There's a soul out there for CNN that
No one knows.
They're real,
True,
Waiting for everything and no one.

When I Think Of

When I think of all the poems I could've written
Instead of chasing or dreaming about girls in my past—
When I consider all the prayers I could've prayed
For all the people who could've used them
Rather than wishing for what I didn't have and didn't
    need—
When I contemplate all the goodness I could've shared
    with others
But chose to pursue vain, vile, or unworthy things,

My spirit slips into murky pools of disappointment and
My heart aches with each arrow of regret that slides
    between the ribs
Of once-solid security.
What foolishness, what rank idleness, what
    wretchedness,
Despite an abundance of love and opportunity all
    around.

Gasping out loud on this trail,
A startled passerby casts a wary glance
At a soul caught in the crosshairs of waste and
    wistfulness.

I could've slipped under the lacy flowers and silent
 ripples
Of Ophelia's brook,
But for the invisible wisps of grace that
Lift up to an unknown tomorrow,
But to a certain destination.

Light and Shadow

Lakeside—
The waves crest white foam,
Elliptical lines to the horizon,
Trapped under a glacier-scarred pyramid,
Wind whipping through ears,
Squinty eyes gazing upward
In vain for the climber friend
Following his boot steps to an
Invisible summit.
Each pause of zephyr coolness
Breaks concentration on the ascent
To a treacherous view
That Muir once enjoyed.
Here, serenity amid the flailing branches
Of ponderosas and firs,
Basking in the radiation from forever.

Except there is no forever on this peninsula,
On this green earth.
Ancient Thousand Island Lake—
What has been forgotten,
What not to be felt again.
Evanescent moment—

Flash, breath, glimpse
Backward into the black hole of memory,
Absorbing every light, every life,
Until we emerge into the
Perpetual Valley of the Shadow
Beyond.

Thousand Island Lake

Plenty, and Not Enough

Here, the Evergreen State has plenty of trees—
Doug firs, red cedar, spruce, cottonwoods even, but
Not enough of the sun shining bright on
Mt. Si or Elliot Bay or even Sequim.
Plenty of rain, mountains, creeks, rivers, bays, sounds—
Water everywhere.
Not enough sprawling meadows, wide-open space, big blue skies
To look everywhere, but
Plenty of start-ups, teriyaki takeout, coffee bars, breweries, wineries even, just
Not enough homes for under $800,000, or wherever today's prices land.
Plenty of homeless people, shelters, donations, gospel missions even—
Though
Not enough sunlight, but
Plenty of beauty and peaks and hiking and biking and skiing and swimming—
Though maybe in a wetsuit.
Plenty of Bibles, and believers, and churches, even the world's Light, still

Not enough of Jesus—but then where is that ever the case?
It's an incredible place, squished into glacial valleys under the volcanoes next to the sea.
Plenty of good reasons to live here,
Just not enough for "home."

African American History Museum

"O, ye nominal Christians! Might not an African ask you, learned you this from your God, who says unto you, 'Do unto all others as you would have men do unto you'?"
—Olando Equiano AKA Gustavus Vasa (1789)

What piercing questions do these Black men and women
Ask of their white masters as they are whipped,
Chained, beaten, raped, killed, and enslaved?
Twelve million forced onto ships, leaving Africa
For the New World.
Only 48 percent make it there alive.
Ninety-five percent of those human beings left wind up
   south of this place—
The Caribbean, Central and South America.
But still—the first slaves arrive in Jamestown one
   hundred miles from here,
One year before the Pilgrims on the *Mayflower*.

Way back, during three years of Virginia history classes,
Why and how were these faceless pioneers and brave
   souls left unspoken?
Of the millions who lived and died in our fair land,
These people cried out over the years, for centuries.

Only two were not forgotten:
Booker T. Washington and George Washington Carver,
Giants of the earth.
Of James Armistead and Prince Simbo, who helped free
   the colonies from British rule;
DC architect Benjamin Banneker (who challenged
   Jefferson on his prejudices);
Pastors Richard Allen, Jarena Lee, and Charles Octavius
   Boothe;
Poets Phillis Wheatley and Lucy Prince.
Writers of power: Solomon Northrup (*Twelve Years a
   Slave*),
David Walker (*Appeal to the Colored Citizens of the World*),
And Frederick Douglass.
Never a word.
Civil War heroes Sojouner Truth and Harriet Tubman;
The 54th Massachusetts Infantry (watch the movie *Glory*
   about Fort Wagner);
Reconstruction legislators Hiram Revels and Robert
   Smalls—
Slipped away from our country's memory for a hundred
   years or more
Before being resurrected.
Was it simply ignorance, a malignant suppression of
   history—or worse?
What dread hands and minds hid these brilliant men and
   women for so long?
Finally, immortal truths are coming out.

Finally, we will meet them in a far better place than this one.§

---

§ For more information on the names listed, check out the museum's website: https://nmaahc.si.edu/.

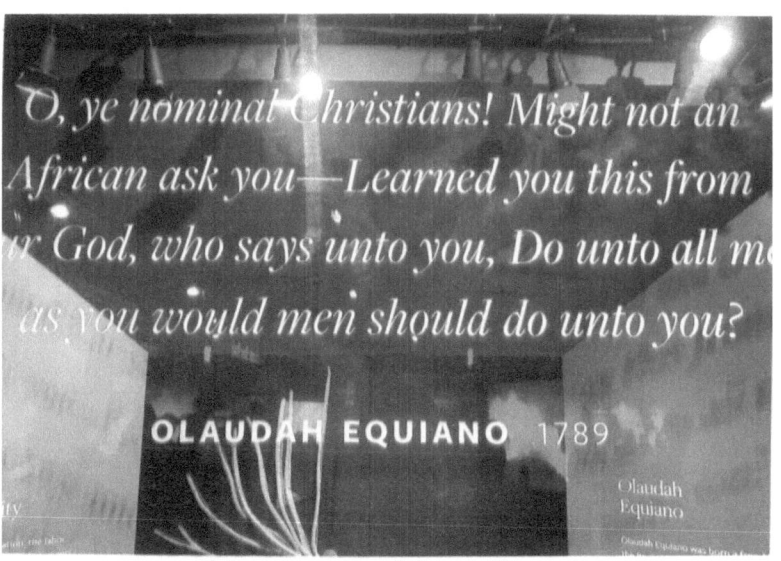

African-American History Museum

Glimpsing Couples

Blueberry Fields Forever

Let me take you down
To blueberry fields, hugging the slough's shore,
The cedar chips crunching into the gooey mud
Until we reach the *tick-tack* of the boardwalks.
We'd hold hands
Past the cattails that wave us on,
To the loamy meadows, strapped down by the lines of vines,
Bursting with Rubels—
Their purplish dimples peeking out from under the rosy
  leaves.

We could lie down among the bushes,
Swallowing the berries you and I gathered,
Lulled by the calls of sparrows and mockingbirds,
Smirking at the rancorous honks of Canada geese.
Your dyed lips dripping with bountiful fruit,
Tangles of twigs mussing your grayish-blond strands.
It would be like the movies—
So peaceful, so far away,
Never again the stacks of deadly bills, toxic payments,
  and threatening messages from
Anonymous sources.
Nothing to get hung about.

You and I could stroll up and down these lanes forever
Along the calm waters—
So distant in time, if not space, from the towers of the city.
A man can see us from there, with good binoculars
Or especially a professional scope, with its crosshairs
Fixed upon my forehead.
It would not be the worst way to go—
Splayed across the wet grass,
Eyes wide open,
Crimson oozing out into the breezy air
Under the too-brief blue skies hugged by grayish clouds,
Where everything is real.

The One I Failed

First friends, and then first love—

You, with the mathematical mind and tennis skills and
    better at German,
More thoughtful, too often biting your lips, analyzing
    situations
Dispassionately.
Me, fretting about the draft, and if you were the one.
Us, a bit adrift studying abroad.

Alone in your dorm room,
Making yourself sick with a whole bag of Äpfeln
Because you'd run out of marks at the end of the month.
You saw through people better than I then, yet

Something inexplicable drew us together—went
Hitchhiking as friends down the Rhein,
Holding the doors of the old man's roadster, blasting
    oompah music at 180 kmh,
Traversing museums and castles and down wooded
    trails together,
Hoisting steins, discussing Hesse and Kafka,
And politics and religion—as if we knew.

Your dorm room—where it began . . . holding hands and
   then more—oh, if.
If only I'd held your treasure more closely,
If I'd taken better care of you—
If only I'd taken care of you and myself.

How many incredibly stupid and painful things did I
   inflict your way . . .
Too many times.
So untrue and hurtful—no excuses there.
Yet you stuck it out as long as you could.
Do you know how many regrets, self-condemnations,
   apologies, recriminations
Have coursed through these veins since then? No matter,
You're the one I failed.
Who knows?

Things are better with me now
(Not that you'd want to know).
I pray so for you too.
There's no telling,
Maybe you've got something far better today.
If only I could've helped along the way.

Sailing

All couples wind up sailing into different seas.
They look curiously at one another
And examine closely the strands of their lives.

Surprised, and ill at ease,
They notice the grain of the wood and the shape of the
    vessel has changed.
Winds pick up, and waves spill over the sides of their
    relationships;
Terrible storms to batter their tiny boat, and then
Who knows?

But even on calmer waters, one or the other mate may
    jump ship,
Diving off the prow proudly or
Slinking over starboard to some other
Far country or unknown depths.

Fairer partners cling to the rudder,
Desperately, together,
Though their craft might run aground on those siren rocks
Or else lie adrift for months in the doldrums,
Waiting for any breeze to move,
To hold on.

Casting for those distant and hopeful coastlines,
Where there's no more steering,
Only finally home.

Look now—how many broken, elated wayfarers
Have made landfall on that celestial shore!

Bedtime Story

You rub your fingers along the lines in my forehead,
Wondering aloud, "What are these here?"
With the biggest smile,
I lie in bed next to you, head in your lap,
While you read your book or do your crossword.
"They're the same wrinkles our daughter Erika has,"
You say triumphantly.
And I smile back
At your face—
Its beauty worn, worn well;
Nothing to reply,
Just cherish this bedtime moment
While we are here.

Te Amo, I Love You, *Ich liebe Dich*

Researchers say there are over six thousand languages,
But I will use only three—
For none of which am I the master.
Te amo.
I love you.
Ich liebe Dich.
The most profound words
One can say to another—
At a wedding, at a sunset, or in a dark place.
You fill my heart full.
Du füllst mein Herz voll.
Llenas mi corazon lleno.
How incredible that such words
Can rip us apart
Or bind one another.
Für immer und für ewig.
Por siempre y por siempre.
Forever and for always.

The Things She Said

You and I are different about the phone.
If it rings and I don't get it,
They'll leave a message.
Don't interrupt,
Let me finish, please;
I know how I feel.
You don't need to explain it to me.
Yes, I do get irritable and cranky,
But just because I'm not liking it
Doesn't mean I don't feel that way.

Forgive me my hard ways,
The ruts of routines.
I am sorry for the pain I have caused.

Perils and Pilgrims

Kennedy Meadows, Sierra Nevada

Last night, I heard a man cry out
From his tent down the meadow—
A voice full of rage, shock, and fear.
I covered my ears with my bag;
I cowered inside.
I didn't think of whether he needed help,
And if I had, I wouldn't have gone.
There was too much darkness between us,
And besides,
It might've been just a mule,
Hysterical about some perceived slight, from a
   chipmunk—
Or a coyote howling
Among those peaks of rock and ice.
The hairs on my neck tingled.
What makes *me* sound like that?
What pain—the loss of a child.

   Before breakfast, scurrying down the trail,
I smelled the smoke before I saw the fire.
The man had made his eyes empty,
The stream rushing by.

Kennedy Meadows, Sierra Nevada

Life Is Not the Silver Comet

Rolling along through the archways of green,
Dappled by light, birds and dragonflies flitting by,
The rhythm of rubber on the asphalt—
Flat, straight, only a few cracks or bumps along the way—
Heading west toward the sun.
You know exactly where you are with the mileage markers
And where you're going
On the Silver Comet.
It's hard, sweaty work pedaling—
Never not worth it.
The fresh air,
The friendly people—
What a great getaway,
Maybe only a flat or a brief thunderstorm to face.
What a break
From our lives as we know them—
Lots of ups and downs, potholes, pitfalls, traps, and terrors,
Crashes, collapses, disasters bound to happen—
Hardly a straight line,
Not toward Alabama or anywhere else.

Evils are lurking on either side
Of this greenbelt refuge.
Oh, but why?
Why can't our lives fit the path of this man-made line?
We yearn for more—
Tell us why this mortal coil is so tightly harnessed
That we must always strain outside of the path,
Not the grunting up the incline,
Rather to face the news, our neighbors,
Our own faces, and our minds and hearts
In the mirror.**

** The Silver Comet is a paved path built on an old rail line between Georgia and Alabama.

Where Have You Been, and Who Are You Becoming?

I knew you back then,
Full of vigor and vinegar,
And so did you,
Bustling to the store,
Laughing with your sisters and brothers,
Scribbling lists and planning get-togethers.
A tad too anxious perhaps,
Still always generous—
At the holidays especially.
We looked up to you, relied on you
For the family dinners,
To pay the tab, or do the cooking.
Patriarch—matriarch.

Now the tables have turned.
(Would it have been better
To have joined the dance sooner when spry?)
Adrift without memories,
Stuck in a room,
Staring at photos of those you cared for
And who now care for you,
Surrounded by helpful staff angels.

You need help getting up from the bed,
Cleaning yourself,
Remembering names—,
Remembering us.
Things are too different.
Soon you'll be even less
What you were then,
Just a shadow
Not at all who you are now,
Hardly a trace—
A thin wisp of hair and string.
Soon, a brighter fire will light
While we sit in the dark and pray
You'll be dancing where
There is no more night.

*For all those I wish I could've known
and loved before they were gone.*

World Demise—Now What?

What happens after Putin overwhelms Ukraine
With his lying, bombing, raping, murdering soldiers,
Leaving nothing but rotting corpses, shattered lives,
Destroyed churches, museums, cities, civilization,
And Europe is left dumbstruck and in terror of
Who will be next.

What happens after China invades Taiwan
With their millions of loyal, silent executioners of
Democracy and freedom,
Only blood flowing freely
Into the South China Sea
Toward Southeast Asia, the Philippines, the Pacific,
And you know where.

Creatures Come Calling

Everyone knows someone who
Keeps fish or snakes for a pet
Though who does that for fun, for real?
How do you "pet" a python or betas or guppies
The way you rub a dog's belly and back,
Scratch kittens and their purring moms behind fluffy ears?
Perhaps there's some second grader somewhere who's
Crying because a lizard or other favorite amphibian
Croaked one too many times,
Though there are a thousand more tears for
Canines and felines headed to animal heaven
Prematurely.

Why does our species go in for cavorting with other
  "lesser ones"
Anyway? How come we go slumming with these lower-
  IQ types?
We've been doing it for thousands of years.
Maybe it's helpful training, in case the roles get reversed
When some other creatures come calling.

A Guide to Middle School, or Heaven and Hell

O, the leaves of grass have turned into weeds,
And instead of flowers, we're stuck with seeds—
Seeds of boredom, sore of whoredom, but
Money without the sex,
Lust without the love,
Eating without hunger,
Drinking without thirst—
Merely a way to pass the time between
Cruelties dealt out blithely from one to another.
An emotionally crippling game of
Too many people with nothing to say,
Too many words with no meaning behind,
Too few saints for all the sinners here,
Too few souls to be saved—
How can you be saved if you think you're all right?
   Don't ask so many questions, or stare so long;
You won't help anybody that way, and besides,
You'll earn yourself a label—
Nerd, slut, fag, wetback, will follow you
Like so many trails of ants,
Spelling out your past, present, and future
For all those who wish to see what isn't
And disinclined to see what really is.

Desert Dreaming

For weeks after camping travels in the Southwest,
His dreams twisted through deserts,
Paused at puzzling highway signs in the sand.

Often, he'd be in a different state each night—
From the salt beds of Death Valley
To the high deserts of the Four Corners
Into surrealistic swirls of slot canyons,
Azure sky peeking through the maroon-pink sandstone
That left him dangling above barely damp river gorges,
The wind and dust always making his eyes squint.

Waking up, his tongue parched,
He'd have to wonder how much longer
He'd have to wander these dusty trails at night.

Death Valley desert

Poetry for People

Poetry Is

Not prose
Not just rhyme
Nor even
Rhythm
Meter
Metaphor
Simile
Symbol
Syntax
Synecdoche
More than
Beauty and horror
Diction
Image
Tone
Love and loss—of course
Personification
Paradox
Consonance
Not even just
Life and death
Allusion
Anaphora

Apostrophe
Couplets
Tercets
Quatrains
Cinquains
  Can't be
Poems
Without
Lighting a way
Painting the world
Breathing fire
Giving air and
CPR for souls

Poem for Poets

Each day, each period, brings you closer to the other side
   of high school—
An even better view!
I am grateful for all the times of sharing, reading, writing,
   learning, laughing
Done together; we did, sometimes, seize the day, didn't we?

Thank you, each one,
For all the brilliant verses you've penned and performed,
And especially last Friday.
Those lines lie on another paper nearby, (live) on my
   phone,
Embedded in this heart,
But my hopes, prayers, and blessings—they do not stay here,
They go forward with you
To the callings and the lands that await you!

What I see in the distance is *steadfast*, it's not . . .
Not the sea, ever-changing with daily tides—
Not the Alps, the Sierras, the Andes, nor the Himalayas,
As lovely and majestic as they are,
Yet their peaks ever so slightly give way to weather and
   gravity,

Not the sky's treasure of planets orbiting and galaxies
    blasting.
The universe is changing every microsecond
And watching us, with lids apart.

It's not our schools, or majors, or jobs,
Which change necessarily with time and growth.
It's certainly not you or me;
We can be forgetful, faint-hearted, foolish,
Daydreaming or bedazzled by the same distractions,
Which scramble everyone else's brains and souls.

What we want isn't steadfast.
When, in blindness, placing hope in what's visible or
    popular
Or in beautiful, momentary, transitory things that fade,
What you want to see is never steadfast.

Steadfast—know and rest in this:
What and who we need is the same . . .
Yesterday, today, and forever.

Go in peace and faith;
You can and will make a difference
In this kingdom and beyond.

Nursery Rhymes and a Broken World

Little Bo-Peep lost her sheep,
And Peter, Peter, had a wife he couldn't keep.
It was a lost world then—
The old world,
Its rhymes creepy, quirky, sexist, and cruel.
With Humpty Dumpty having a great fall,
With London Bridge falling
Down, falling down,
And Jack falling down the hill
With Jill tumbling after.
A distorted cruel world
With talking animals and flying spoons and mean souls.

No surprise—the verses and
Times were particularly rough for the fairer
Sex, and their little ones.
Women who had so many children,
They didn't know what to do.
Old Mother Hubbard
With empty cupboards,
With the wind blowing,
The cradle will be falling
And down will be coming

Baby, cradle, and all.
When Georgie-Porgie kissed the girls and
Made them cry
(Or die),
Even the little girls . . . so bad, they were horrid.
Such a distorted cruel world back then,
So it is now.

As hard and mean as those rhymes on us were,
How do today's films, shows, books, and TikToks fare?
That piglet crying *wee-wee-wee-wee* all the way home,
Away, far away—all of us long to escape this dome of dread.
Instead,
We keep going 'round and 'round and 'round the mulberry bush
Until there's a fix, if at all—
Whenever that may be . . .
Shhh

Souls/Sanctuary

Skulls on Fence Posts

Middle of October, the neighbors have already
Put out their pumpkins,
Hung out their harvest banners;
Scarecrows dot these cookie-cutter blocks.

But now the white-sheet ghosts and the lime-colored witches
Are creeping into the ostentatious display,
Giant spiders and their webs soon to follow.
Papier mache gravestones teeter over sidewalks.
How can one send mere children into this nightmare?

No problem, it's the twenty-first century.
Let's electrify everything—
Flashing lights, smoke smearing the sunset sky,
Remote sporadic gurgling belching across lawns
From unseen monsters crawling toward their prey.

Meanwhile, the lady down the street
Is nailing shrunken heads onto her fence
While her friend stands back and helps to line them up evenly.
What are we doing here?

Are we merely banking on immortality,
　　Flouting Death's plans for our demise.
Dante didn't dispute that,
Though revealing things far worse
Down past the River Styx.

Or is there something even more dismal in this show—
Paddling upstream, whistling through the churchyard
To a hollowed-out rendezvous with the Evil One.

When Marlow first sees the knobs on the railing
Around the compound Kurtz has erected at the Inner
　　Station,
He assumes they're "ornamental"
Instead of the grinning skulls of would-be "rebels."

From suburbia to the uttermost ends of the earth,
Leading into the heart of an immense, horrible darkness.

Skulls on Fence Posts

No Turning Back

Sometimes, the tide goes out on a certain thing,
And it's not coming back ever again.
Our God is one of abundant blessings—
Extravagant, unexpected—
Yet even He will not undo time,
Taking the pain, sorrow, sin of the past,
And transforming them—yes.
Still, some things sit in the rearview mirror forever,
Reflecting what could've been but will never be.
Oh, grace sometimes is just getting you through the day.
One heart can have so many pieces,
And there are so many hearts.
May it be enough that we do not sit frozen in our tears
   forever.

Ash Wednesday

Outside the stifling sanctuary, I could still hear the drone of
"Repent, Believe, Obey" in the flooded parking lot,
How the liturgy spoke of sins we tremble to mention,
And we trembled.

The bread of flesh lies dry,
Barren, without the soaked harvest of sacrifice.
Consecration and celebration are too gentle to describe
That anguished blood-letting.

Pierce the dragon of Self through;
Mortally wound the heart that strays;
Bury it in the black cave until
The new dawn.

Violent words and actions
To be shied away from
By those too caught up in
Wisps and webs of gentle deceit.

Whose hand hangs in midair?
The gleaming glint of the sword
Catches the eye and waits.

Gracious

We must've taken a dozen of
Ubers while visiting loved ones in South Africa—
Drivers from "Joburg" and "KZN" and "Zim."
The one who stands out most is
Gracious—the only woman driver.
Cheerful and talkative and mother of
Three children—twenty, sixteen, and twelve—
Who'll likely need to join others going back to Zimbabwe
 soon.
South Africans think they're taking too many jobs away.
Like many drivers, she complained of high petrol costs
 and trying to earn a living.
We talked about the ANC and Ramaphosa's problems
 with corruption in SA and how
We also have our problems with corrupt presidents in
 the US.
She asked me who the best American President was, and
I said, "Abraham Lincoln—
He freed the slaves and led our country through a civil
 war and died doing it."

Gracious talked most to me on the ride about her ex-
 husband—

So unfaithful with so many women,
Took her money and wasted it,
Left her with the children.
She prayed, prayed though kept
Visiting fortunetellers, who took her money.
They promised he'd return,
But he never did—no matter how much she paid or how she cried—
Even thought about doing herself in.
Finally, she stopped trusting in charms and curses and the ex.
Gracious told God He'd have to be the only one to help.
She'd been double-minded, and now she's at peace.

We talked about faith and prayer
I told her she was doing what
Psalm 37:3 says:
"Trust in the Lord and do good."
Gracious turned around as we stopped at Zoo Lake
And asked,
"Can you please say that Psalm again?"
I told her and closed the door and
Walked away.[††]

[††] Note: "Joburg" = Johannesburg; "KZN" = KwaZulu Natal, a province in South Africa; "Zim" = short for Zimbabwe; "ANC" = African National Congress, the ruling party; "SA" = common abbreviation for South Africa.

37,000 Feet

Flying over Utah, Nevada,
The Sierras in the distance,
Above White Mountain
Where Dad traipsed around
The oldest living trees on earth
With me after Mom died.
We're over that now—
Glorious peaks, shining
With snow in the sun.
Grandeur, majesty, beauty, and
Now glory—waiting to embrace
You now, Dad.
Heaven's gates beckon to
Ever greener, everlasting fields of
Wonder, awe, amazement—and
Love.
Streams and rivers and oceans of
Love, for you and for us all.
Jesus has you,
Now and forever.

"But as it is, they desire a better country, that is, a heavenly one. Therefore, God is not ashamed to be called their God, for he has prepared for them a city."
—Hebrews 11:16

Dad by Ancient Bristlecone Pine Ranger Station

Margin

Unlike with school binder paper, margin is
Usually where things need to happen.
A pencil-thin pink line marking
On the edge of sea and sand.
Constant thrumming of energy to and fro;
Skin must mediate the germs and sunlight of the world
To organs beneath.
Doorsills and gateways full of traffic
Heading somewhere;
The borders between us and what's not.
Edging the lawn of our world,
The space between malignancy and life,
Between victory and defeat,
Between soul and body.
The thin yellow line on the highway,
A threshold between life or death.
Where is the margin between flesh and the soul within?
Avoid gravitating toward one or the other;
There is space in between,
For there is a kind of kingdom there.

Electing to Depart

We're checking out of the Evangelicals;
We're heading out the door.
It's been quite a ride.
Would like to say thanks,
But no,
We're getting out of here.

Open the door, get out of the way,
You can keep heading your own direction,
As long as we're not there.

We can't get out quick enough;
Not sure where that'll be.

Not sure where you are going.
Though it can't be good, it's
Away from the destinations
You espouse.
How bitter that you've bought in
And traded your good news for a chance
To break bread and share a table with
One who shuns and shames it.

Somehow the caravan toward the other kingdom got sidetracked;
Some extra stops along the way.

Once you pointed us to a bright shining star, sharing the way,
Inviting us in . . .

But it's over now, it's done for sure.
Don't know where you're going;
Wherever it is—we'll not be there.

Compromised Couriers

Walter Brueggemann says that
We are compromised couriers of the Gospel;
Tainted messengers of hope in a desperate world.

Just look at how Rebekah and Jacob deceive Isaac,
Hairy fur and special food for a blind man
Cheating Esau out of his birthright and blessing—
Turnabout is fair play:
See how the trickster Jacob is
Tricked in turn by Uncle Laban,
Leah for Rachel, for another seven years.

And then poor Leah—four babies yet no love;
Beautiful Rachel—love, but a barren womb.
And on and on . . .
The forefathers were so conniving, distorted, sinful
  to the brim;
These become the patriarchs (and matriarchs) of the
  Chosen People.

Up to today:
Carry on that twisted tradition, despite your best
  intentions.

What have you not done, at least in your head?
Is a pure heart or clear conscience necessary to embrace
    the blessing?
Who then could come to the table—
Embrace and celebrate, though not one of you has clean
    hands.

Just ask:
Free the children, the grandchildren, and beyond—
From the prison yard of your past.
The God of Impossibles
Holds Impossibilities in His hands;
Even the life everlasting
For a soul like you and yours.

Beyond the Mirror

Ode to Superheroes

When I was in grade school, most everyone wanted to be
Superman—leaping over tall buildings, faster than a
Speeding bullet: blah, blah, blah . . . but the Flash
   fascinated
Me. I loved to run, though ever so slowly in football
And everywhere else. Later, ever so slight, I grew long
   hair,
Bearing no resemblance to Samson—and no Delilah.
By the '90s, Batman was the "In" hero; Heath Ledger
Nailed that as his nemesis, until Marvel unraveled
The longest list of superheroes the world's ever seen.
Now everyone's all about Wolverine, Spider-Man,
   Thor—
How did God, even a Norse god, get much play in
   movies?
Who's more likely: Elijah the fire maker or Marduk
Exhuming himself from beneath the Tigris-Euphrates?
Me—I'm waiting for the One who can die and live again.

My Friend Chuck

Several people told how my friend, elder, life group
  leader
Chuck explained why he became a special-ed teacher.
Long ago in the Philippines, he'd met Eddie,
An older student, with a cigarette in his mouth,
Hunchbacked, full of warts—and learning problems.

Years later, Chuck dreamed of encountering heaven,
But still teaching in a classroom.
A beautiful person approached him: "Hey, Chuck!"
And gave him a big hug.
Chuck needed to know who this person was
Who said, "Don't you recognize me? I'm Eddie!"

Many people, many memories;
Time to say good-bye last night at your service,
Time to say good-bye last Wednesday night in your
  bedroom.
Your eyes closed, your labored breathing, your hospice
  nurse,
Our pastor Tim there by your side.
I got to see you and pray for you again, just one of
  thousands for you—

"This light and momentary affliction is
   preparing for you an
Eternal weight of glory beyond compare."
Though you had to squeeze through that difficult door
With much pain over several years, and many tears,
Still you had a soft landing in the arms of Jesus.

Your principal told the memorial service today
That he found notes for the other staff in your desk the
   day after you died.
No surprise—Scripture verses about
Persevering, and hope, and the "eternal weight of glory
   yet to come,"
Plus this precious line:
"God created me for a relationship with Him—how
   amazing is that?"

It was a long way, and I worried and prayed about how
   long it would take you to get through the door to the
   other side.
But you were—and now I am—
Confident in that very same hope:
A person we both know,
Now and always.

At a Loss for Words

Do you ever have a day when no matter what
You can't ever say anything right?
At the church get-together or the faculty meeting,
There are serious topics being addressed, so
You strive to share something meaningful or important,
And the faces look back at you, go blank, and the conversation moves on
Around the table as if you'd never uttered a word?

   Or just talking to the neighbors, listening to
   your spouse,
About the real issues of their days.
People deserve attention and support;
You intend to show empathy but
Then come across patronizing or superficial
And they walk off shaking their heads (perhaps inwardly), and
You're not sure why.

   Despite all your best intentions and efforts
You feel a bit, or more, of a schmuck.
Everyone at the party heads out laughing,
Clasping each other by the elbows or hugging;

You hang back a few steps,
Knowing no one knows you're there.
Though you'd like to contribute,
You know already it's not for you today.

Looks and Souls

They say that beauty is only skin deep—
Though it can run deeper:
Inside the beauty herself and in eyes of her beholders.

Of course, most of us trundle around with plain faces,
Noses protruding, bent, or worse,
Body askew as if a blind welder
Had fastened it all together.

Just take a look around the airport
The next time—what an amalgamation of body parts
Out of sorts, which makes people out of their minds.
   If you've got bread, you get shredded
And full of plastic parts.

We're not talking about those
Laden with deformities or missing limbs,
Confined to wheelchairs.

These souls often convey
A chilling reality beyond
The comforting allure of
The eyes, the lips, the silhouette.

Those who are lovely beyond words,
Shaking their locks
And taking a look in the looking glass
One last time before—

Beauty is a gift for the few who enjoy it for a time;
Souls are gifts for all, for all time.

Long Road to Mortality

(with thanks to Douglas McKelvey)

Life may be a long road to mortality,
And still more a preparation for
The way ahead.
A foretaste of better days to come
The best of times, of Time itself.
True—
Each of us must be squeezed through that
Exceedingly narrow gate into which our souls are
Pressed, like virgin olive oil or extraordinary wine,
Pressed such that these skins and shells
We call bodies are peeled off,
A necessary part of the process—
Often slowly and painfully, though at
Other times all at once with a
Almost-electric jolt and yet—
To rejoice at
The shock of homecoming,
Better than the best surprise party ever . . .
Let us prepare ourselves—
For it's coming,

Sooner or later.
   May our minds and purposes be focused;
The gift of each blink of the eyes
Taste its flavors today.
Cherish each moment with loved ones
While they and we are passing through.
Even in the midst of strife and grief,
Revel in the longing for
The ultimate.
Surely our hearts can ring like chimes even now
In anticipation of what is coming, and who.

A Love Song for Beulah and Maida

How I long to have met you both,
Though each of you died a decade or two before
　my birth,
Leaving my parents bereft in their childhood of one who
　would always
Love.
As I play with my own grandchildren, I think what an
　attenuated connection over years, and miles, and
　tragedies.

What names! Have I ever met another person with
　those ever?
Maida, an "unmarried girl"—and Beulah in Hebrew was
　a "married woman" . . .
Maida, your eyes shine out and teeth protrude a bit, just
　like Dad's, but I will never see them outside of these
　black-and-white photographs.
Beulah, your stoic demeanor, is that really your
　personality, like it was our mother's—or was it the
　colon cancer already growing inside, even then?
How much I could show you now—of my wife, our
　children, your great-grandchildren!

But not now, not yet—not until we cross over to
the other side.
I feel the pull that way, the longing for something
more real.
We'll be coming for the Real Us then.

Two Women Portraits

Births and Deaths

June is the month for weddings, they say.
In our world, four beloved babies arrived
   this past month:
Two grandsons, then a late girl for the pastor, and a
   preemie for a teacher.
Each a cherished life
Despite the long, sleepless nights of wailing.

Who would not give their own life so that one could live?
Breathing is not always a given.

Over there is a bereft soul who just
Suffered her third miscarriage and so
Yearns and mourns for a child to carry and love.

The same month: three souls near our
Hearts but in different places
Left this earth once and for all.

A beloved sister, a loyal neighbor, a young man much
   too young—
Tears so little.

Someday,
Each of these newborns will have to squeeze through that
Other passageway,
Sooner—or let's hope—much, much later.

There's a dim light over the horizon—
Is it slowly fading or just starting to brighten?
Let's trust in the latter.
All of us will meet up again,
Else all is lost.

Standing at the Fountains

*For Joaquin and Zion, each grandson born on a
different day and on a different continent in June 2022.*

While we stand together in this
Modern-medieval Tuscan village and
Casino in the heart of South Africa,
Joaquin loves to stare
At the water pouring into the pools and
Listen to the dripping
Plops, one after the other.

He holds tightly, with his five-month-old
Hands, onto my index finger—
It's reassuring to both of us
And a miraculous joy for me.

Just like he does
At the fountain inside the gates
Of the community
Where he and his parents live.
Of course, he can't talk yet or
Walk or crawl or even quite sit up.
He chews on his finger, my index finger, his toes.

Soon, that will all change.
May we still hold each other
(Long after then
Without hanging on or clinging)
Even just in our hearts.

Faces and Lights

Have you ever been captivated by a
Smile, a look, on another's face that's so
Incredibly disarming, without guile, and
Brings so much
Instant instinctive pleasure to
See?
From what place does that come?

We're not talking the sophisticated glamor of Hollywood
   queens (or kings)—
No Elizabeth Taylor (or Cleopatra), Halle Berry, David
   Beckham,
Penelope Cruz, or Scarlet Johansson, or Brad Pitt, or
   Maria Sharapova.
Just the person at the grocery checkout or standing
   in line.
You have to try hard not to stare;
Looking twice is okay, maybe, but no more—
That would be creepy

And yet—
People are not their appearances,
Not their clothes or faces or bodies,

Whether beautiful or plain,
Youthful or aging.
Why are we so disarmed, enamored by the looks that will surely fade?
The gorgeous exterior covers, even fools,
The eyes and the minds of both beholder and their temporary occupant,
Hides the core of what lies beneath.

The radiant joy, a heart of love, the wisdom beyond age,
Not clothed in resplendent, dazzling beauty—
Immortal horrors or everlasting splendors.

> *"It is a serious thing to live in a society of possible gods and goddesses, to remember that the dullest and most uninteresting person you can talk to may one day be a creature which, if you say it now, you would be strongly tempted to worship . . ."*
> —C. S. Lewis

One Day, or 10,000—No Matter

Live as if your life depended on it.
Be mindful of each moment;
Be mindful of each person, especially
Those you love—always remind yourself
You have much to learn about them, from them.

Be purposeful; you are only for a time.
Squeeze the most of each moment
And still be at peace—calmness and focus work well
Together for others, and for you.

Listen. It's not easy to do it right.
Listen more than talk, and with
Patience. There is so much to learn, and
Others have much to gain from your ears.
Share—when needed, when it's time.

Smile often, forgive often, judge only
If required. You rarely know why people
Do what they do.
Pray for them instead—it can make a difference.
And remember to forgive yourself.
Rejoice always. It's a good preparation

For what's to come after this life.
Walk, run, bike, go into nature whenever you can.
Keep writing—some good things are created
That weren't there before.

Love abundantly. It's a free gift
If you believe, and it's free to give to
Others. Keep loving each day.
Live.

About the Author

Steve Kennedy has been in education in a variety of places in the US and overseas for over forty years. He currently lives near Atlanta, Georgia. This is his first book.

www.ingramcontent.com/pod-product-compliance
Lightning Source LLC
Chambersburg PA
CBHW020543080526
44583CB00013B/978